NOTES

including
- *Life and Background*
- *Introduction to the Works*
- *Critical Discussions of* Player Piano; The Sirens of Titan; Mother Night; Cat's Cradle; God Bless You, Mr. Rosewater; Slaughterhouse Five; Happy Birthday, Wanda June; *and* Breakfast of Champions
- *Special Topics*
- *Review Questions*
- *Selected Bibliography*

by
Thomas R. Holland, Ph.D.
University of Nebraska

INCORPORATED
LINCOLN, NEBRASKA 68501

Editor	Consulting Editor
Gary Carey, M.A. *University of Colorado*	*James L. Roberts, Ph.D.* *Department of English* *University of Nebraska*

ISBN 0-8220-1352-5
© Copyright 1973
by
C. K. Hillegass
All Rights Reserved
Printed in U.S.A.

1991 Printing

Cliffs Notes, Inc.   Lincoln, Nebraska

CONTENTS

Vonnegut Notes

LIFE AND BACKGROUND

Kurt Vonnegut, Jr. was born in Indianapolis, Indiana, on November 11, 1922. His father and grandfather were architects, and his family had a tradition of pacifism and atheism — two intellectual traditions which were to figure prominently in his works. He was educated in Indianapolis and first began writing as a reporter for the Shortridge High School *Daily Echo,* the first daily high school newspaper in the country. He entered Cornell University in 1940 as a biochemistry major and soon began writing for the student newspaper. Despite his pacifism and his German-American background, he volunteered for military service in 1943 and was sent by the army to study engineering at Carnegie Tech. He then transferred to the infantry and served as a scout during the Allied invasion of Europe. He was captured by the Nazis and was in prison in Dresden when the Allies bombed the city — an incident which is mentioned in several of his novels and is the major setting of *Slaughterhouse-Five.*

After the war, Vonnegut entered the University of Chicago as a graduate student in anthropology. During this time he married Jane Cox, a childhood sweetheart. He continued his journalism career, working part-time as a reporter while at the University of Chicago, but when his master's thesis was rejected by the school, he abandoned both journalism and anthropology and became a public relations agent for General Electric in Schenectady, New York. In 1950, after three years with General Electric, he quit to devote his full time to writing; his first novel, *Player Piano,* is partially based on his experiences in the corporate world.

Vonnegut's first three novels, *Player Piano* (1952), *The Sirens of Titan* (1959), and *Mother Night* (1961), met with little success.

He kept himself and his family alive during this period by writing short stories of uneven quality for popular magazines. His third novel, *Cat's Cradle* (1963), was never a best seller, but it developed an "underground" reputation and began to be especially popular on college campuses. By the time *God Bless You, Mr. Rosewater* came out in 1965, Vonnegut had developed enough of a following that the book sold well and it was widely reviewed. His next novel, *Slaughterhouse-Five* (1969), was both a critical success and a runaway best seller.

Having made his reputation as a novelist, Vonnegut turned to the theater in 1970, with *Happy Birthday, Wanda June*, a revised version of a play he had written years before under the title *Penelope*. The play ran for 142 performances off-Broadway and was moderately successful with the critics. In 1972, he wrote a play for the National Television Network, *Between Time and Timbuktu, or Prometheus-5*. This was not so much a new work as a series of scenes from his novels and plays, strung together with a connecting plot. Also, *Welcome to the Monkey House*, a collection of his short stories was issued in 1970, a volume which included stories from an earlier collection, *Canary in a Cat House*.

Vonnegut's latest novel as of this writing—which he claims will be his last—was published in 1973. *Breakfast of Champions* is a recapitulation of the major themes of Vonnegut's earlier works and is a farewell to his characters, whom he frees in the Epilogue, much as Thomas Jefferson freed his slaves. The book has met with a great deal of critical and popular acclaim; if Vonnegut is indeed abandoning his writing career, he is leaving it on a note of triumph.

INTRODUCTION TO THE WORKS

This volume is a study of the major works of Kurt Vonnegut, Jr., eight novels and a play, all published between 1952 and 1973. Vonnegut is also the author of a television script, two collections of short stories, and numerous uncollected stories, articles, and interviews.

In each of his novels, Vonnegut's vision of the universe has remained consistent. He depicts man as a puppet, a powerless victim of forces he does not understand. Man is driven to try to find order and purpose in his life, but he is doomed to failure, for there is neither order nor purpose in the universe. Any meaning which man sees is an illusion that he has created for himself. Sometimes these illusions are pleasing and harmless; sometimes they become disastrous.

Vonnegut's first novel, *Player Piano* (1952), depicts a futuristic automated American society which has been divided into two classes: those who run the factories and those who do not. The protagonist of the novel is an engineer who becomes dissatisfied with social conditions, but finds himself powerless to change them. Instead, he becomes trapped between the opposing forces of revolution and reaction and is forced to make a choice between them. After vacillating between the two alternatives for some time, he chooses to side with the revolutionaries. But he realizes, finally, that he has been used: the revolution was not a serious attempt at improving society; it was merely a symbolic action in which he served as the primary symbol.

The Sirens of Titan (1959) is a science fiction fantasy novel which makes a serious point about man's dissatisfaction with his situation and his powerlessness to change it. In this novel we first find Vonnegut's depiction of the universe as a mechanistic chaos which has neither the order nor the purpose which man feels he must find in it. The protagonist, Malachi Constant, is cruelly used by Winston Niles Rumfoord, who has gained the ability to foresee the future. But Rumfoord is, in turn, being used by beings of a higher order of power from the planet Tralfamadore. And even the Tralfamadorians are not really in control of what happens in the novel. Constant is shuffled back and forth among the planets of the solar system in pursuit of an elusive destiny which Rumfoord has foreseen. At the end of the novel he finds that his life has been meaningless and pointless and that its only redeeming quality has been the love which he did not obtain until it was almost too late.

Vonnegut's most "realistic" novel, the only one not to include any elements of science fiction, is *Mother Night* (1961, 1966). It is supposedly the autobiography of a Nazi war criminal, Howard W. Campbell, Jr. Campbell served as a propagandist for the Nazis, but was also an American spy, broadcasting coded messages to the Allies. He acted not out of any belief in what he was doing, but simply for the sake of playing the roles imposed on him. In effect, he was being used by both the Germans and the Americans. The main action of the novel occurs in New York in 1961, when Campbell's true identity is revealed by a Russian spy. In the ensuing crisis, Campbell finds that he does not really know who he is, or what purpose his life has really served. Finally he surrenders himself to Israeli authorities for trial; shortly before he is to be brought to trial, he hangs himself. His life has long since ceased to have any purpose, and what purpose it did have was imposed on it by others.

Cat's Cradle (1963) is a surrealistic fantasy of the end of the world. It takes place mostly on the Caribbean island of San Lorenzo, where a bizarre new religion called Bokononism has sprung up. The novel satirizes both religion and science as means of codifying man's knowledge. The two systems are antithetical: religion is based on satisfying lies, while science deals with horrifying truths. As the novel ends, it is a scientific discovery, a new form of ice which melts at a high temperature, which destroys the world. Man is caught between the extremes of religion and science, left to work out their contradictions for himself. Religion finally seems the more satisfactory alternative, simply because it is more humane, but since neither is an accurate description of the real nature of the universe, one must choose the more useful.

God Bless You, Mr. Rosewater (1965) deals with the attempts of an eccentric millionaire, Eliot Rosewater, to do his part toward establishing a Utopia. Rosewater commits himself wholeheartedly to the task of loving and helping others. But his unselfish love of humanity comes into conflict with the selfish love of others — the individualized love which his father and his wife feel they deserve from him. By making love general and universal, it becomes meaningless; only when it is personalized and reciprocated does it fulfill its purpose. The novel deals with this paradox and with the effects of selfishness for material things — specifically, Rosewater's money. The novel concludes with Rosewater's leaving the family fortune to those he has tried — and failed — to save through love; thus he keeps it from falling into the hands of greedy relatives.

Slaughterhouse-Five (1969), Vonnegut's best-known novel, combines the horrors of war with the fantastic escapism of science fiction. The hero, Billy Pilgrim, has "come unstuck in time" and is moving spasmodically from event to event through his life in random sequence. The central event of the novel is the massive bombing of the city of Dresden, Germany, during World War II, while Billy was a prisoner there. Billy moves back and forth — from the nightmare of prison and bombing to his peaceful life as an optometrist in Ilium, New York, and the fantasy of being mated to a movie star named Montana Wildhack in a zoo on the planet Tralfamadore. Billy is, to a great extent, a perpetual victim of circumstance, but he learns from the Tralfamadorians to accept his life as it is — because he has no power to change it.

Vonnegut's play, *Happy Birthday, Wanda June* (1970), is a study of popular concepts of heroism. The main character is a soldier of fortune and a big game hunter, Harold Ryan. He has been missing for eight years, and his wife has become engaged to a pacifist doctor. He finally succeeds in defeating his enemy, but finds that in the process he too has been defeated. The play is a mixture of realism and fantasy, with scenes in Ryan's living room being commented on by characters who are dead and in an absurd "Heaven." By treating death lightly, Vonnegut manages to impress upon the audience that death is a serious matter and, in the process, he questions a code of values which treats a killer, like Harold Ryan, as a man to be admired. He also questions the

values of the pacifist, who is willing to risk his life for his principles. In the end, the play seems to say that the only real value
is life itself.

Breakfast of Champions (1973) is a wildly comic, deeply
pessimistic investigation of American culture. The plot centers
on an encounter between two men, science fiction novelist Kilgore Trout and Pontiac dealer Dwayne Hoover. One of Trout's
stories is the catalyst in driving Hoover insane, sending him on a
wild rampage. But the plot, which is slight, is really of only sec-
ondary interest in the novel. The real hero is the author, who is
working out the basis of a new culture for himself, while he dis-
cards the old. And what he is discarding of the old culture is the
main subject of the book, which is composed of advertising
slogans, graffiti, crude drawings, and much of the rubbish of
American popular life. The satire in the book is corrosive, but
the author is, finally, cautiously optimistic, for he believes that
he has discovered a basis for a new set of values, based on the
sanctity of all life. Vonnegut says that this book will be his last
novel, and it is, in part, a recapitulation of his former themes,
ending with his setting his characters free.

Vonnegut's "freeing" of his characters in this novel is a final
resolution of one of his major themes. Throughout his writings,
his characters are plagued by a lack of free will. All of his protagonists have been puppets, controlled and manipulated by
others, or by fate. And, as a novelist, Vonnegut has, in effect,
been the puppetmaster who controlled their movements. In re-
leasing them from his control, he is asserting their right as individuals to live free of manipulation. Yet this resolution is ironic,
for Kilgore Trout, the character to whom the author announces
his intentions, is not satisfied with free will. He wants to be
given youth. Presumably, man will never be satisfied with his
lot.

DISCUSSION OF INDIVIDUAL WORKS

PLAYER PIANO

Player Piano, Vonnegut's first novel, is based on his experiences as a public relations man for General Electric from 1947 to 1950. It is a "futuristic" novel, like Orwell's *1984* or Huxley's *Brave New World*—that is, Vonnegut takes specific trends in contemporary American society and depicts the sort of society which these trends might develop into. Thus he is able to simultaneously criticize certain aspects of his society and to warn against what might happen if these divisive elements in society were given free rein.

In the world depicted in this novel, American society has been split into two unequal parts. The Second Industrial Revolution—the use of computers and programmed machines—has eliminated human labor in industry. All the work, even the planning, is done by machines. At the top levels of society are the engineers and managers who program and run the machines; no one else is of any social importance. All those who do not belong to this elite class have two choices: join either the Army or the Reconstruction and Reclamation Corps (sarcastically called the "Reeks and Wrecks"). This social structure is reflected in the layout of the city of Ilium, New York, the setting of the novel. The north side of the Iroquois River is divided between the machines and the homes of those who operate them. The rest of the city's inhabitants live in Homestead, on the south bank of the river.

There is little contact between the inhabitants of the two banks of the river. Such contact is openly discouraged because of the fear that saboteurs from Homestead might disrupt the working of the factories. The people of Homestead, it is clear, are not content. Their material needs are taken care of; the main computer, EPICAC, determines what goods they need and programs the factories to produce these goods in the exact quantity necessary. But the Homesteaders are denied human dignity by the system. They are given, according to their I.Q., menial jobs which keep them busy without giving them the satisfaction of feeling they are accomplishing anything worthwhile. The nickname "Reeks and Wrecks" implies what the members of the corps are — the dregs of society. The army is little better; its business is largely drilling and training, keeping men busy with petty details. Because of the fear of rebellion, soldiers are not permitted to handle real weapons unless they are sent overseas. And the men in the army yearn for a war because it will give them the feeling of doing something constructive.

A few of the people of Homestead manage to preserve their dignity by escaping categorization. Alfy Tucci, for example, develops an innocent con game by learning to identify songs on television with the sound turned off. Alfy's talent is pointless, of course, but it is a way of escaping society's restrictions, of making a living by his own devices. As such, it is a mild form of rebellion, which foreshadows the futile revolution with which the novel ends.

Alfy's attempt to drop out of society also illustrates the major theme of the novel — man's attempt to preserve his individual identity despite society's attempts to make him conform. And it is not only the Homesteaders whose individuality is denied them through social pressure to conform. The chapters which take place at the Meadows, the resort kept for meetings of the engineers and managers, illustrate the mindless conformity which is imposed on even those at the top of society. Even among the elite, we discover, there are malcontents. Doctor Garth, for example, destroys the Oak, the symbol of the company's unity; Doctor Harrison openly expresses his contempt for the Meadows; Doctor Finnerty quits his government job to become a leader in the revolt of the Homesteaders. These, however, are minor rebels; the novel centers on one particular rebel and his relationship with society — Doctor Paul Proteus, a man trapped between two hostile worlds.

Proteus's father, Dr. George Proteus, was the chief social architect of the Second Industrial Revolution. As National

Industrial, Commercial, Communications, Foodstuffs and Resources Director during the war, he reshaped the American economy and society in their present forms. Paul himself helped in this operation. He, his friend Edward Finnerty, and his chief rival, Lawson Shepherd, were in charge of programming the Ilium Works for automatic operation, making computer tapes of the movements of especially skilled workmen. Shortly thereafter, the workmen themselves were made obsolete after the machines were programmed to remember the men's movements.

Dr. Proteus has now risen to the position of manager of the Ilium Works and it is expected that he will rise further. He is being considered for the position of manager of the Pittsburgh works, the most important managership in the company. But despite his success, Paul Proteus is discontent with his life. He has been unable to adapt completely to his role in society, unable to unquestioningly accept the necessity of the divided nature of society, and unable to believe that the materialistic basis of his culture is absolutely good. Early in the novel he finds himself, by chance, in a bar in Homestead; here, in his conversation with the common people in the bar, his doubts about society become magnified. He begins to see the spiritual squalor in which the people of Homestead live; he begins to realize that his elite class is perpetuating the misery of the rest of society. But at the same time he realizes that he is powerless to change anything. His wife, his social position, and the promise of social advancement all serve to keep him from acting to correct the evils of society. Before he can act, he must have a catalyst to start him moving.

Doctor Proteus finds his catalyst in two people—his best friend, Edward Finnerty, and a man he meets in the bar in Homestead, Reverend James J. Lasher. Finnerty has risen through the ranks more rapidly than Proteus and is a member of the National Industrial Planning Board, a committee which controls government policy. Finnerty is even more of a malcontent than Proteus. He has always refused to conform to the behavior expected of him, and he clearly has destructive tendencies, which extend even to suicide. But these tendencies are directionless until he meets Reverend Lasher; his only major action until now has been to resign from his job.

Reverend Lasher, the prime moving force behind the rebellion, is in many ways a puzzling character. He is a man of God, a dedicated and sincere opponent of what he considers evil. Yet he is a cynical and bitter man, willing to use others to his own ends, often cruelly. For instance, he pointlessly torments Proteus with the false story of his son's suicide and, later, he is responsible for capturing and imprisoning Proteus so that he can be used as a symbol for revolutionary activities. He arouses the people to revolt against the machines and against the structure of society, knowing full well that the revolt will fail. But, for him, the rebellion is a success. It was done "for the record," as a testimony to the value and dignity of the individual. For Lasher, the revolution did not have to succeed; the fact that it was attempted is evidence of the power of the individual against mass society. He is less interested in actually altering the nature of his society—in the end, he does not seem to believe this was ever possible—than in making a symbolic gesture for the struggle of good against evil. Even though he does not triumph, the gesture itself is a sort of victory in its affirmation of the spiritual independence of the individual.

Paul Proteus's motivation in siding with the rebels is a sincere desire to right the wrongs of society. He shares neither Finnerty's cynical, destructive tendencies nor Lasher's hopeless moral idealism. He believes—wrongly, as it turns out—in the real possibility of altering the world through positive action. He arrives at this position gradually, only after all other alternatives have been closed to him. His main complaint against the social system is its cold, unfeeling inhumanity. Vonnegut graphically illustrates this aspect of society in his opening chapter, relating how Proteus's cat is "automatically" killed by the electronic guard system at the factory. Proteus's reaction to this incident is the reader's first clue that Proteus is emotionally unsuited for his job.

Proteus's discontent is increased during his first visit to Homestead, where he meets a living "ghost," Rudy Hertz, the craftsman whose movements were recorded on tape during the first stages of automation at the factory. In effect, Hertz is still running the machines, as a ghost, but his body goes on living in Homestead, out of a job and hopeless. It is also in the bar in Homestead that Proteus finds the player piano from which the book takes its name. This instrument is analogous to the automated machines in the factory: it is played by the "ghost" of the man who originally punched the rolls which activate it. The piano plays a significant symbolic role in the development of Finnerty's character; during his evening in the bar in Homestead, he plays it, replacing the "ghost" on the piano rolls with a living performer. This illustrates the humane ideals of the rebels as opposed to the impersonal technology of the managers.

Throughout the novel, Proteus is never able to act with free will; he is continually placed in situations in which he has no choice. His first impulse, when faced with the evidence of the social evils he has been guilty of perpetuating, is to drop out of society. He buys a farm, with the idea of quitting his job and living off the land. But this idea is abandoned because of his wife's staunch refusal to go with him. Then, at the Meadows, his supervisor, Kroner, makes his advancement in the company dependent on his agreeing to become a spy, infiltrating the organization which his friends Finnerty and Lasher have organized. He never firmly decides whether or not to join the "Ghost Shirt Society" — named after a religious society of American Indians — or to function as Kroner has suggested, as an espionage agent for the company. Such a decision is forestalled when he is drugged in Homestead and held captive by Finnerty and Lasher. Proteus is needed by them as a symbol. As the son of the founder of modern society, his word in their support is valuable to them. But again, before any real decision can be made, he is recaptured in a police raid and is held in prison. It is here that he finally decides that his mission is to be leader of the Ghost Shirt Society, and he publicly confesses that he is. During his trial, the rebellion breaks out and he is briefly freed. Only after the rebellion has failed, when he realizes that he was the only one of the ring-leaders who expected it to succeed, does he realize how he has been used by both sides in their struggle against each other. He was caught in the middle—and there was no middle ground. Thus his choices were not really made by himself, but by forces which controlled his actions. During the trial, he is described as a marionette, a puppet on a string. This has been his function throughout the novel—not to act, but to react, to behave in the way which those around him prescribed.

Proteus's major flaw is his inability to adapt to the world, as those around him do. He cannot alter his beliefs and values to suit the situation, and he is not entirely sure what he wants. He has to be what he is, rather than becoming what is required of him. In this respect, he is contrasted with old Luke Lubbock, who is able to change his identity by changing his costume. To a lesser extent, Lasher and Finnerty resemble Lubbock because they are adaptable. They have choices to make; Proteus does not. Early in the novel, it is noted that Finnerty could have been anything he wanted, while Proteus had to be what he was. In this sense, Proteus's name is ironic, for he is named after a mythological figure who could change himself into any form at will. The mythological allusion functions in another respect: the fictional Proteus was able to see into the future and tell the truth about it; it is exactly this that Paul does at his trial, much to the dismay of the judges.

In the final analysis, Paul Proteus is not so much a hero as he is a victim of circumstance. He is a man who is forced to choose between two undesirable alternatives and finds that he has been stripped of his free will and left only those choices imposed on him by others. This is a constant theme of Vonnegut's writings: man finds himself manipulated by forces beyond his control; thus his actions are dictated by chance, rather than by conscience.

THE SIRENS OF TITAN

More than any of Vonnegut's other novels, *The Sirens of Titan* is a science fiction fantasy. The world described in this novel is based on improbable premises of scientific discoveries which alter man's perceptions—both of himself and of the universe—and Vonnegut makes little attempt in the novel to blend this fantasy world with the everyday world of present reality. Yet in its themes and ideas, *The Sirens of Titan* is really quite similar to the author's other novels. (Moreover, the references to time-travel and to the planet Tralfamadore anticipate the use of these fantasy elements in later novels, such as *Slaughterhouse-Five.)* The main theme of this novel is man's inability to control his own destiny, even when he has foreknowledge of what is to occur. This theme is presented by recounting the adventures of a victim of chance, Malachi Constant.

Constant's story is told chronologically, from his first meeting with Winston Niles Rumfoord to his death at a bus stop in Indianapolis years later. Yet the major events of the novel are all foreshadowed in his initial conversation with Rumfoord. Rumfoord acquired his knowledge of the future by flying his private spaceship into a chrono-synclastic infundibulum, a funnel-shaped field of energy in which all time is simultaneous and all contradictions are resolved. At the moment of his entering the infundibulum, Rumfoord begins to exist simultaneously at all times and places which the infundibulum touches. All moments of his life exist at once; he is able to see the future because he is living it at all times. All of time has always existed for him—and always will exist.

This notion of time causes some problems in interpreting the novel. For one thing, this ordering of time implies some sort of predestination—a patterning of events before they happen. Yet Rumfoord makes it clear that this is not the case, by insisting that existence is a state of chaos. It is merely a random sequence of events, with no particular pattern. There is no reason for things occurring as they do; it is simply that each moment is structured according to the events which occur within it. The structuring of the moment is inalterable. There is no foreordained purpose in the existence of the universe (though, as we shall see, some parts of existence do have an unsuspected purpose).

Another difficulty with Rumfoord's infundibulation is that it seems to give him a great deal of power over ordinary human

beings. Yet this is merely the appearance of power. Like everyone else, he is bound to perform according to the way particular
moments are structured. He has no more free will in the matter
than anyone else. He is the architect of a war between Earth and
Mars and he is the founder of a new religion; to a great extent,
however, these are things that happened *to* him, rather than
things which he accomplished. It is clear at several points in the
book that Rumfoord is not enjoying his role in history, but he
knows that he is powerless to alter any of it.

Vonnegut's protagonist in the novel, Malachi Constant, is
little more than a pawn in the cosmic game of which Rumfoord
has become the unwilling ringmaster. The events in Constant's
life are, in reality, only the closing moments of a process which
began some 200,000 years before, when the spaceship of Salo, a
Tralfamadorian messenger, broke down on Titan, one of the nine
moons of the planet Saturn. Fifty thousand years of human history have been a series of messages to Salo that his replacement
part is on the way, and Constant's purpose is to bring the part to
Titan with him, in the form of his son's good luck charm.

Salo is eleven million years old and, like all Tralfamadorians,
is a machine. (Vonnegut gives a different description of Tralfamadorians in *Slaughterhouse-Five.*) Salo's mission was to carry a
secret message across the universe, as far as Tralfamadorian technology could take him. He did not know the contents of the message and was instructed not to open it. Eventually he disobeys
his orders and opens the message, at Rumfoord's request (though
Rumfoord is removed to a different part of the universe before
Salo can show it to him). The message contains a single word:
"Greetings."

But for all the pointlessness of Salo's mission, Malachi Constant goes through almost unbelievable torments in carrying out
his mission — that is, delivering the part for the spaceship. His
troubles begin when he is invited to meet Rumfoord during one
of Rumfoord's "materializations" on Earth. Rumfoord appears on
Earth according to the motions of the chrono-synclastic infundibulum once every fifty-nine days, always in private, at his home

in Newport, Rhode Island. Constant is the first person from out-side the estate with whom he speaks since flying into the in-fundibulum. Many others have applied to speak with him and have been turned down; now Rumfoord asks that Malachi Con-stant be invited.

During the interview, Rumfoord tells Constant that he will visit Mars and Mercury, return briefly to Earth, then go to Titan. He also tells him that while on Mars, Constant will mate with Rumfoord's wife, Beatrice, and that they will have a son named Chrono. Beatrice Rumfoord has been told the same story and, like Constant, has tried everything in her power to keep the prediction from coming true.

At this time, Constant is the richest man in the world, but he soon finds that, through a series of bad decisions and reversals of luck, his fortune is wiped out. Shortly thereafter, he is kidnapped by a pair of Martian agents and taken to Mars to serve in the army, which Rumfoord is training to invade Earth. On the space ship to Mars, during a bout of drunken boasting, he rapes a woman who turns out to be Beatrice Rumfoord.

Chrono, the son of Malachi and Beatrice, is born on Mars, as Rumfoord predicted. But his father is not to know him until years later. Constant and Beatrice are separated after the rape, and like most of those kidnapped and taken to Mars, their memories are "cleaned out" so that they do not know who they are or what has happened to them.

In the army of Mars, Constant is known by the nickname "Unk." He differs from most of his fellow soldiers in that al-though he, too, has become essentially a machine controlled by radio signals, he continually fights against his condition by try-ing to remember the past and trying to assert his individuality. The most significant incident of Unk's stay on Mars is that he is forced to murder his best friend, Stony Stevenson. Although Unk does not remember the incident later, Rumfoord uses it against him later as moral blackmail.

The army of Mars is being trained, under Rumfoord's direction, to invade and conquer Earth. Yet this is not really the purpose of Rumfoord's plan; the invasion of Earth is only the opening phase of Rumfoord's design to bring to Earth a stable society founded on peace and human equality. For all his noble purposes, however, it is indicative of Rumfoord's cynicism that he is willing to sacrifice thousands of lives in the cause of peace. The ill-fated Martian attack is repulsed by the Earthlings and most of the army is killed immediately. When the truth about the attack becomes known—that those killed were fellow Earthlings —many of them women and children—there is a general revulsion against war. The surviving Martian invaders, Bee and Chrono among them, are treated as martyrs and given special status in society.

Constant, however, does not get to Earth immediately. Rumfoord has the ship carrying him and a soldier named Boaz misrouted to Mercury, where Constant remains for three years. Rumfoord's purpose is to prepare the groundwork for Constant's return to Earth, Constant being the central symbol in a new religion. The Church of God the Utterly Indifferent teaches that all beings, living and dead, are brothers. God does not care about them and it is up to them to care for themselves. It is considered a crime for any man to have any advantage over another; natural advantages are offset with "handicaps" of one sort or another. Meanwhile, Rumfoord has prophesied that a straggler from the army of Mars, called the Space Wanderer, will appear on Earth. Also, a sort of devil symbol has been devised—a doll called a "Malachi," which is attached to a hangman's knot. An effigy of Constant, it represents the unfair advantage which the rich and powerful had during the previous centuries of human history. Thus, ironically, Constant is symbolically both the devil and the Messiah of Rumfoord's new religion.

Vonnegut treats the Utopia which Rumfoord has created as a mixed blessing. On the one hand, it is a system of peace and equality, the first which Earth has known, but it was achieved at the expense of individuality. Everyone is required by law to be equal with everyone else, and this imposed absolute conformity obliterates the characteristics which distinguish individuals, making everyone merely a part of a homogeneous mass society. Furthermore, the reign of peace and benevolence has been achieved only through the slaughter of the "Martian" innocents. Thus it would seem that Rumfoord, the "saint" who accomplished all of this, is an absolute cynic, manipulating others to achieve his own ends. But it must be remembered that Rumfoord himself has no real power. His only power lies in his ability to foresee what will happen; he has no power to alter it. He, too, is subject to the forces of chaos which govern events; like everyone else, he is "a victim of a series of accidents." Even the Tralfamadorians, who have exerted some control over the course of human history, are victims, if on a higher level. They, too, are unable to alter significantly the course of events which they envision. Their manipulation of the "Universal Will to Become" is a significant source of power, yet even they are not in complete control. The breakdown of Salo's ship is one indication of this. And even being a machine does not save Salo from "human" failings—that is, a lack of self-control. Salo is powerless to prevent his friend Rumfoord from being removed from the solar system. And though he is able to give the dying Constant an illusion of an afterlife, it is only an illusion. He is powerless to prevent Constant's death; he can only make it a little more pleasant.

   The Sirens of Titan is Vonnegut's first detailed exploration of the question "What is the purpose of human life?" And for those who demand a clear-cut explanation, he supplies one: we are part of a plan by the Tralfamadorians to deliver a missing part to Salo's space ship. But the question itself is meaningless, for, Vonnegut implies, the purpose of life is life itself. The only rewards are the rewards of life itself; to look for more is foolish. Constant's life is an emblem of this hopeless quest. At the beginning of the novel, he has everything a human could want, yet he is dissatisfied. Chance teaches him a lesson by taking away what he has and alternating him from world to world, making him a symbol of the foolishness of human aspirations. Yet even Constant receives a reward: in the last year of his life, after years on Titan, he finally falls in love with Beatrice. This is the one thing he has never had—a feeling of emotional involvement with another human being. This, it would seem, is the most precious possession of all.

MOTHER NIGHT

The hero of *Mother Night*, Vonnegut's third novel, is a man who has been "dead," metaphorically speaking, and who briefly returns to life. By his own account, Howard W. Campbell, Jr. has been "living in purgatory," in a state of suspended animation, from 1945 to 1961. The novel, which except for some prefatory material is told in the first person, is cast as the personal memoirs of Campbell. The story concerns events in three timeframes: the time spent during Campbell's imprisonment in Israel; the time immediately prior to his arrest by Israeli authorities; and the time during and immediately after World War II. The "fictional present" of the novel, the time from which events are narrated, is during Campbell's imprisonment in Israel, in 1961. From this perspective, Campbell tells of the events which led to his arrest, which constitute the main plot of the novel, and of relevant events which occurred in Germany during World War II, when he was simultaneously a Nazi propagandist and an American intelligence agent.

The main concern of the novel is Campbell's dual identity. And, in fact, it is really a treble identity, since Campbell sees himself primarily as a poet and playwright, a romantic dreamer whose true inner self is never touched by the plots and schemes which his external personalities are involved in. He quotes, toward the end of the book, a trite phrase from a television program: "Howard W. Campbell, Jr. — this is your life!" But he might, more appropriately, have substituted another phrase: "Will the real Howard W. Campbell, Jr. please stand up?" For his memoirs are, above all, a search for his true identity, an attempt to reconcile and come to terms with the three parts of his self.

In the Editor's Note which prefaces the memoirs, Vonnegut gives the reader a key to the three parts of Campbell's identity.

As a writer, Vonnegut says, Campbell was accustomed to lying "without seeing any harm in it." Especially as a playwright, he was accustomed to manipulating reality, to creating false appearances for the sake of the show. As Campbell himself points out, he accepted his intelligence assignment not out of any moral conviction—in fact, he maintains a high degree of moral neutrality to the end—but because he was a ham. Publicly, he played the role of the strutting Nazi propagandist; privately, he played the role of the American secret agent, broadcasting messages he did not understand to an audience unknown to him. But neither role ever meant more to his "true self" than a part in a play; he did not care that the "play"—World War II—had the highest moral and historical consequences for the world.

Campbell's perception of his own moral neutrality is not shared by others. To the world at large, he was one of the most vicious of the Nazi racist propagandists. His role as an American agent has never been made public. Ironically, Campbell's two closest friends are also role-playing; the painter George Kraft and "Helga," the woman he believes to be his long-lost wife, are leading double lives: Kraft is actually Colonel Iona Popatov, a Russian agent, and "Helga" turns out to be another Russian agent, Campbell's sister-in-law, Resi Noth. They have been assigned to kidnap him so that the Russians may use him for propaganda purposes. In fact, most of Campbell's life has consisted of his being used by others, for their own purposes: first, by the Nazis and the American government; then, by the Russian agents, and, finally, by American agents attempting to break up simultaneously a Russian spy ring and a neo-Nazi organization in New York City. Like most of Vonnegut's protagonists, Campbell is acting not because of his own volition; instead, he is being made to react to the machinations of others.

The person most responsible for using Campbell in the last year of his life is his neighbor, George Kraft, who was the first person to break through Campbell's self-imposed isolation. It is Kraft who sets the complex machinery of Campbell's "resurrection" in motion. He contacts Russian intelligence agents to set up Resi's disguise as her sister Helga. He sends word of

Campbell's existence to Campbell's greatest admirer, Dr. Lionel Jason David Jones, D.D.S., D.D., publisher of a scabrous neo-Nazi hate sheet, *The White Christian Minuteman.* And he notifies the man who considers himself Campbell's archenemy, Bernard B. O'Hare. The only moment of glory in O'Hare's otherwise pointless existence was his capture of Campbell at the end of World War II; his absolute hatred for Campbell has become a guiding light to his life. And it is as a result of O'Hare's futile confrontation with him that Campbell finally determines to surrender himself to Israeli authorities. So Kraft is ultimately responsible for everything that happens to Campbell after his "return to life."

Yet Kraft is an unlikely person to be cast in the role of manipulating Campbell's fate. He is an old man whose main interests in life are chess and painting. (In fact he is to become, after his imprisonment, one of the most influential painters of his day.) He is also a very inept spy—the American agents who arrest him reveal that his organization is staffed entirely by American counterspies. Like Campbell, he seems less committed to his official duties as a spy than he does to his private interests. In fact, his friendship with Campbell seems to be more genuine than his political interest in him. He and Resi—who is no better a spy than he is—conspire to rescue Campbell from their own plot to kidnap him so that the three of them may escape together to live in peace.

Campbell describes Kraft's ability to remain his true friend—while cynically using him—as "schizophrenic"; indeed, all three main characters of the novel—Campbell, Kraft, and Resi—seem to share this sort of schizophrenia, an ability to dissociate the motives and actions of one part of the self from those of another. Kraft determines to use Campbell only after their friendship has developed and he learns who his friend really is. Resi, on the other hand, becomes involved in the plot to use him because she has long been in love with him and wants to be with him. Like Campbell, they are able to contain contradictory impulses and motives without attempting to resolve them; also, like Campbell, they are actors, able to subordinate their private identities to a conflicting public role.

Despite their schizophrenic tendencies, however, Campbell, Kraft, and Resi are not insane. In this respect they are contrasted with Reverend Jones, with his associates, and with Adolf Eichmann, whom Campbell meets in prison in Israel. These men exemplify what Vonnegut, speaking through Campbell, describes as the "classic totalitarian mind," which is attuned to a logic all its own. This kind of mind is not totally insane; it is able to function normally in most situations. But it has the peculiar power of being able to rid itself of facts and ideas which it considers inessential and move, in Vonnegut's description, like "a cuckoo clock in Hell." The missing truths are like teeth removed from the gears of the clock, and it is these missing truths that account for the insane logic of a Jones, or an Eichmann, or the society of Nazi Germany. Campbell, Kraft, and Resi are aware of their contradictions; Jones and Eichmann are not.

It is even implied in the novel that this "schizophrenic" ability to overlook contradictions is a necessary factor for mental health. Campbell opens his account by describing his four guards in the Israeli prison, each of whom has somehow adapted his image of the world to suit his own requirements. One, an expert on ancient Israeli history, knows nothing of the atrocities recently committed against his people by the Nazis. A second, while a prisoner at Auschwitz, volunteered for duty in the *Sonderkommando,* a duty which meant almost certain death. A third managed to conceal the fact that he was a Jew and served in Hungary in the SS, the Nazi secret police. The fourth was the hangman of the Nazi war criminal Rudolf Hoess and treated this duty matter-of-factly, as if it had been an everyday occurrence. Each of them has adapted his image of the world to accommodate the absurdity of his own life, and their descriptions stand at the beginning of the book as a foreshadowing of Campbell's adaptations to his own absurdities.

Such adaptations based upon illusion are fragile, and Campbell's are shattered when his "Blue Fairy Godmother," Frank Wirtanen, discloses to him that Kraft and Resi are Russian agents. Even with this knowledge, however, Campbell has nowhere to go but back to them, to await the raid by the G-men whom

Wirtanen tells him about. Even an illusion of love and friendship is better than nothing, and in the ensuing conversation with Kraft and Resi, Campbell finds that their love and friendship are something more than an illusion. During the raid, Resi's world is similarly shattered when she discovers that the man she loves does not correspond with her idealized vision of him. And when Campbell cannot give her any further reason to live, she poisons herself.

Set free once more by Wirtanen's intervention, Campbell finds himself incapable of action. He "freezes"; he cannot move — simply because he has no reason to move. He cannot choose a course of action because there is no basis for a choice. He has nothing left to live for. And he notes that, during all his years in "purgatory," he was kept alive by curiosity; now even that is gone. He has arrived at the point of existential crisis — when the things which kept him alive are no longer sufficient. He is briefly shaken out of this mood by his encounter with O'Hare; because of his inability to cross the pool of vomit which O'Hare leaves in the hall, he finds himself making a decision. He knocks at the door of his neighbor, Dr. Abraham Epstein, and asks to be delivered to the Israeli authorities for trial.

Dr. Epstein wants nothing to do with Campbell's request; he would rather forget the war. But Epstein's mother casts the deciding vote, not out of vengeance, but out of pity. She recognizes in Campbell the state of mind which led men like Andor Gutman, Campbell's guard in Israel, to volunteer for the *Sonderkommando* at Auschwitz — a state of absolute passivity in which one desires nothing but self-extinction. Yet Campbell is not even choosing suicide; in surrendering himself to the Israeli authorities, he is leaving the choice as to whether he shall live or die to others. His physical catalepsy is simply an outward manifestation of his inability to make any decisions.

Campbell is finally forced to choose for himself between life and death when Wirtanen discloses his identity as an American spy to the Israeli authorities — and Campbell chooses death. The book closes with his determination to hang himself "for crimes against himself" (a play on "crimes against humanity"). His decision is not so much a moral judgment on his role as a war criminal as it is an admission of this infidelity to himself. In his role-playing, he lost sight of his real self and lost his free will. And having never known real freedom, he finds the prospect of being a free man "nauseating." Only in his love for Helga was he ever really free; and, even then, he substituted a self-centered individual love for a love of mankind. His "Nation of Two" with Helga allowed him to ignore the realities of the world, allowed him, as Vonnegut warns in his Introduction, to become what he pretended to be.

Ironically, Campbell's suicide is his first really free act in the whole novel. Throughout, he has permitted himself to be used by others—first, by the Nazis and by the American intelligence agents; then, by Kraft. Now that he is free, and able to choose for himself, he chooses to escape the onus of free will once and for all.

CAT'S CRADLE

In *Cat's Cradle*, Vonnegut focuses more closely on the theme of illusion and reality, a theme which he explored in his previous novels. The moral which Vonnegut finds in *Mother Night* could be even more closely applied to this novel: "We are what we pretend to be, so we must be careful about what we pretend to be." Throughout the novel, we find illusion—even illusion which is not seriously intended to deceive anyone—becoming reality. The artificial structures which man imposes upon chaos to explain reality to himself tend to become fact, and once the rules of the illusory game become established, they may not be violated. Indeed, they become, for all practical purposes, incontrovertible truth.

It is a very gloomy world which is depicted in the novel, one which is perhaps best characterized by a chapter from *The Books of Bokonon* entitled "What Can a Thoughtful Man Hope for Mankind on Earth, Given the Experience of the Past Million

Years?" The chapter consists of a single word: "Nothing." Yet for all its bleak pessimism, the novel is wildly, at times almost insanely, funny. The plot is episodic; there are nearly as many chapters as there are pages in the book. Each chapter relates a separate incident or a fragment of a conversation; nearly all of them end in a joke, or a bitterly satirical comment, or both. The effect is like that of a demoniacal comic strip in which we move spasmodically from frame to frame, from punch line to punch line.

The story is told chronologically, from a "fictional present" of the last few chapters of the novel. The narrator is the chief protagonist of the novel and is therefore limited in his perceptions by virtue of being within the story himself. Some aspects of the narrator's role in the novel are established in the allusive opening sentence, "Call me Jonah." This is a parody of the opening sentence of Herman Melville's *Moby-Dick*, "Call me Ishmael"; as such, it carries into *Cat's Cradle* some of the symbolic overtones of both *Moby-Dick* and "The Book of Jonah" in the *Old Testament*. Like *Moby-Dick*, this novel is an investigation of the nature of good and evil and a chronicle of a quest for truth, for meaning in life. Like Ishmael, our "Jonah" (whose real name is John) plays the role of a detached observer of the major conflicts of the novel throughout most of the story (though he does become involved in the main action late in the book); and Ishmael and "Jonah" are the final, symbolic survivors of shipwrecks, though in *Cat's Cradle* it is not merely the *Pequod* which has been destroyed—it is the world.

The narrator resembles Jonah of the Bible in that he is working God's will without understanding what end he is serving. In fact, his purpose seems to be completing a book he once began, entitled *The Day the World Ended*. The title of the original book was overstated; it was an investigation of the bombing of Hiroshima. But, ironically, that title applies much more suitably to *Cat's Cradle*, for the book "Jonah" ends up writing is literally a description of the events leading to the end of the world. It is as if, like the original Jonah, the narrator strayed from his real purpose, and God, through the workings of *zah-mah-ki-bo* (the

Bokononist word for "inevitable destiny"), has renewed the narrator's sense of purpose. Jonah's mission in the Bible was to prophesy the destruction of the city of Nineveh; our modern Jonah's mission seems to be to witness and chronicle the destruction of the world and serve as a final, ironic symbol of man's defiance.

The novel is an investigation of good and evil and a man's search for truth. Yet, in the framework of the novel, these are misleading terms: good and evil, truth and falsehood—these are illusory. They are merely aspects of the central theme of illusion and reality. This theme, and its sub-themes, are developed in the book through a satirical comparison of the "truths" of science and the "truths" of religion, with a constant emphasis on the moral principles embodied in each.

Vonnegut's investigation of science centers on two of its technological developments: the atomic bomb and the fanciful "ice-nine," ice which has a melting point of 114.4 degrees Fahrenheit. Both are the products of research done by Dr. Felix Hoenikker, who becomes a subject of the narrator's research while working on *The Day the World Ended.* Dr. Hoenikker, who has been dead for some time, is described by his children and his associates as having been a peculiar person. His whole life seems to have been involved with his work; he had no need or desire for human companionship. The only memory anyone has of his ever trying to communicate with his family was when he attempted to play "cat's cradle" with his midget son, Newton. Cat's cradle, which becomes the central metaphor for illusion in the novel, is a children's game in which a piece of string is manipulated with the fingers into patterns; the main pattern vaguely resembles the shape of a small, cat-sized cradle. There is no real cat or real cradle involved; it is merely an illusion which requires a great leap of imagination to see any connection with the reality which the name implies. For Newt, this is the most horrifying experience of his life; his father, who has no experience in dealing with people, tries to badger him into seeing what is not there. This incident is important in establishing, early in the book, the theme of illusion and reality. Newt's consequent psychological problems are a symptom of his inability to see reality in another man's illusion.

Dr. Hoenikker seems, in many ways, to be a product of arrested development. He is the most brilliant scientist of his time, yet he has no social graces whatever. He regards his work as play and is unable to sustain any serious interest in it once the aspect of play is over. Much of the work of his subordinates involves trying to keep him interested in what he is doing, finding ways to make his work into a game to keep him interested. He is, in fact, an overgrown child who has no concept of any social or moral importance in what he is doing. After the first atomic test, a co-worker says to him that science has now known sin; his response is to ask, in all seriousness, "What is sin?" And when told by a secretary that God is love, he asks, "What is God? What is love?" These are terms which, as a man of science, he cannot understand; they simply do not rationally compute.

Yet Vonnegut is doing more in these scenes than establishing Dr. Hoenikker's eccentric character. Dr. Hoenikker is responding as a scientist; science has no room for morality because morality is not a rational concept. The research scientist is not responsible for the uses to which the products of his research are put; once he is finished with them, that is an end to the matter. Dr. Hoenikker bears no guilt about the deaths of the people in Hiroshima; nor would he accept responsibility for the end of the world because of his invention, ice-nine. According to him, the scientist's business is to discover the truth about natural phenomena; the use to which this truth is put by the rest of mankind does not concern him. His only goal is the advancement of pure knowledge (which Dr. Breed describes as "the most valuable commodity on earth"), not its application.

The matter of using science for human benefits is dealt with in one of its most obvious forms, medicine. The chief character in this regard is Dr. Julian Castle, a man who has rejected his earlier life as a millionaire playboy in order to devote himself to fighting a futile battle against disease and death in the Republic of San Lorenzo in the Caribbean. (It is an assignment to interview

Castle that leads "Jonah" to his ultimate destiny on San Lorenzo.)
But though Castle's deeds are admirable, his sayings are usually
bitterly cynical; his character seems to be a mixture of Albert
Schweitzer and Groucho Marx. Dr. Castle seems to believe in
nothing whatever, to have no informing moral code by which he
determines his behavior; yet he is a truly "good" man. His partner at the House of Hope and Mercy in the Jungle, as he calls his
hospital, is an even stranger case. He is Dr. Schlichter von Koe-
nigswald, a former staff physician at Auschwitz. Dr. von Koenigs-
wald is "doing penance" for the lives he destroyed in Nazi
Germany; by Julian Castle's estimate, he should break even
around the year 3010. Here we have a case of a "monster" who
has become, of his own volition, a good man. Yet he professes no
moral beliefs; he professes to believe only in science. The behavior of these two men is patently absurd; they are not acting
out of any deep convictions in sacrificing their lives for others.
They are simply doing what they are doing, for no real reason
whatever. And the absurdity so evident in their lives also exists
in the lives of those who act according to their principles, scientific or religious. Principles, it would seem, are meaningless,
and man does not really have ultimate control of his actions. As
Bokonon puts it, "We do what we must"; a man is what he is and
has no choice in the matter.

Religion is satirized in the book in the form of Bokononism,
a "pack of lies" (foma) invented by a Negro named Lionel Boyd
Johnson, who set himself up as a holy man living in the jungle.
Bokonon's "religion" began, like most things in the book, as a
game. Johnson and a deserter from the U.S. Marines named Earl
McCabe were cast up by the sea on San Lorenzo after their boat
was wrecked. The island was in a state of anarchy simply
because no one wanted to govern it; it was not worth the trouble.
Bokonon (the San Lorenzan pronunciation of "Johnson") and
McCabe set about to establish a Utopia on the island, but found
that this was impractical. There was no way of raising the stand-
ard of living above abject poverty and squalor. So a game was
invented in order to take the minds of the people of San Lorenzo
off their misery. McCabe played the cruel dictator living in the
city; Johnson played the benevolent holy man and prophet living

in the jungle. McCabe outlawed Bokononism ("to give the game more zest") and thus the state of moral anarchy was divided between good and evil, as a game. But the illusion which Bokonon and McCabe created rapidly became reality. McCabe became an insanely cruel dictator, persecuting anyone suspected of Bokononism; and Bokonon, much to his own surprise, became a saint. Despite the fact that Bokonon continued to insist that his religion was nothing more than a pack of harmless lies, intended to divert the people's attention from their misery, his religion thrived. Everyone on the island was a Bokononist, despite the threat of execution, being impaled upon a huge iron hook. Bokonon's lies became, as Vonnegut tells us, like the lies of writers, "the most beguiling form of truth." Cynical as the truths of Bokononism were, they gave the people of San Lorenzo something to elevate them spiritually and relieve them of their physical misery.

The God of Bokononism is, like the God of the religion founded by Rumfoord in *The Sirens of Titan,* "utterly indifferent." He does not care about the Earth; he created man solely for the purpose of admiring the rest of creation. He is surprised at man's insistence on life's having a purpose and meaning, and he leaves it to man to find purpose and meaning for himself. He has no intentions, good or evil, toward man; he simply leaves him alone, to fend for himself.

In a contradictory tenet of his religion (and Bokonon cheerfully admits contradictions), Bokonon insists that mankind is organized into teams which work God's will. A team is called a *karass,* and no one ever knows who else is in his personal *karass,* or what its purpose is. Any conscious organization of human beings — fraternal orders, countries, or other categories — is a *granfalloon,* or a false *karass.* (The Crosbys, who insist upon being identified as Americans and Hoosiers, are notorious *granfallooners.*) The narrator, at the end of the novel, realizes what the purpose of his *karass* has been: to bring him to the top of Mount McCabe, bearing a symbol, while the world dies out. He automatically rejects the symbol which Mrs. Crosby has prepared, a homemade American flag. But just as he is puzzling over this matter, he meets the dying Bokonon, who gives him his symbol. It is to be the narrator himself, frozen to death by ice-nine, thumbing his nose at God (referred to as "You Know Who"). This is the final absurdity of the novel: a meaningless gesture of defiance, delivered to the god of a religion which admits that he is a lie, who—if he does exist—will, Bokonon tells us, "only smile and nod." It is a futile gesture if there ever was one, but one that the narrator has to make.

In comparing religion and science, then, Vonnegut finds them almost diametrically opposed. Science propounds a "truth" based upon hard, cold facts. It has no connection with the important business of living, of leading a moral, dignified, and purposeful existence. Religion is concerned with these matters, yet its "truth" is founded on lies. It does not increase human knowledge, as science does; if anything, it ignores it. But it gives man a way to live, a means of interpreting reality for himself. It does not matter that this interpretation is an illusion or that the illusion is more pleasing than the reality which lies behind it. Science is amoral; it does not recognize good and evil. Religion must make these arbitrary distinctions in order to give man a means of formulating a code of ethics. Vonnegut's satire of religion is harsh, but in the final analysis, religion emerges as more attractive, in this book at least, than science does.

The only saving grace of humanity seems to be, as in *Mother Night* and *The Sirens of Titan,* love. And Bokononism, like all religions, offers love. The absurd ritual of *boko-maru,* the "intermingling of souls" (soles) by putting feet together, is an expression of love. And unlike sexual love, *boko-maru* is not meant to be monogamous. It is extended to everyone. The beautiful Mona Aamons Monzano berates the narrator, after his sexual advances have been repulsed, for wanting all of her love. True love is not to be given to one individual alone; if it is to be effective, it must be shared by all mankind. The narrator's mistake is wanting exclusive love, not universal love. He seeks only to gratify himself, rather than to identify with and help others. Love, like the laughter offered in the book, may not solve any problems, but it does make the ordeal of living less painful.

In the process of his investigation of illusion and reality, Vonnegut calls into question the fact of man's understanding the universe and himself. "Man is vile, and man makes nothing worth making, knows nothing worth knowing," Julian Castle remarks. Bokonon tells us that man must question, must ask "Why?" But man can find no answer, only illusion: "Man got to tell himself he understand." Man cannot *really* understand, however, because there is nothing to understand. There is no meaning or purpose in the universe—or in human life. All order and purpose that man sees is nothing more than a cat's cradle, an illusion of a non-existent reality. There is, as little Newt puts it, "No damn cat, and no damn cradle."

GOD BLESS YOU, MR. ROSEWATER

The main character of *God Bless You, Mr. Rosewater,* according to the narrator, is a sum of money. And indeed it is this sum of money, the principal endowment of the Rosewater Foundation, which motivates all the action in this parable of materialism. Except for a relatively minor character, Norman Mushari, the lawyer, there are no human characters manipulating others; rather, the manipulation in the plot is a result of the influence of money upon the lives of those whom it touches.

The Rosewater Foundation was created as a means of avoiding taxes on the money by Senator Lister Ames Rosewater of Indiana. The capital is managed by the Rosewater Corporation, and all officers of the Foundation—direct descendants of Senator Rosewater over twenty-one years of age—are to be permitted to live on the profits of these investments, without touching the principal itself. The first President of the Rosewater Foundation is Senator Rosewater's son, Eliot, who in 1964, the time at which the main action of the novel takes place, is forty-six years old and is widely considered to be insane. The story concerns the quixotic way in which Eliot manages the Foundation and the efforts of Norman Mushari to have Eliot declared legally insane so that the money might be transferred to Mushari's clients, Eliot's cousins. Mushari's real purpose, of course, is to make his own fortune on the legal fees resulting from such a large transaction.

Eliot's "madness" manifests itself in a peculiar form: it consists of wholly and uncritically loving everyone he comes in contact with. He proudly paints the Foundation's motto on the windows of the shabby, second-floor flat in Rosewater, Indiana, which is the Foundation's headquarters: "How Can We Help You?" And he attempts to live according to the unselfish attitude conveyed in the motto by living as simply as possible and devoting all of his energies to helping others. Ironically, despite his vast wealth, his "help" usually consists merely of giving friendly advice and being willing to listen to others' problems. His financial transactions on behalf of the Foundation are few and small. The people he is helping, whom his ultra-conservative father considers—perhaps accurately—as the hopeless dregs of society, do not need money so much as they need affection. Their hopeless situation does not arise from their poverty, but from the feeling that society has cast them out and has no use for them. Eliot, in offering to care for them, is giving them what they need. And while his father and the family's attorneys consider him a madman, the people of Rosewater, Indiana, consider him a saint.

Eliot's behavior is a result of perceiving the effects of chance upon an individual's life. What differentiates him from the people of Rosewater, Indiana, is that he was born into a family that had an estate of millions of dollars. He describes this situation with a metaphor: he and others like himself are permitted to drink at the Money River, either as a birthright or as a reward for their skill and cunning in financial dealings. But they are not permitted to slurp so loudly that they attract attention of others, thereby giving away the location of the Money River. Most important, those who are permitted to drink are given rank, privilege, and dignity; these benefits are not shared with the rest of mankind. Thus Eliot sees his real function to be restoring a sense of dignity to the people among whom he chooses to live. He does not do this so much by sharing his wealth—at least not initially—as by offering them uncritical love.

Eliot's love, however, is a kind of paradox in the book: is it really used to help others, or is it, as his father suspects, a form of self-gratification? Is Eliot genuinely pleased to see others happy, or is he pleased because he is able to make them happy? These conflicting attitudes are expressed in the graffiti in the hall leading to Eliot's office — two poems by William Blake, one written there by Eliot, the other by his father. These contradictory poems illustrate the contradictory attitudes which Eliot and his father have toward love. Eliot considers love to be something shared with everyone, regardless of their circumstances. His father believes that love is a precious gift to be granted to only those closest to you. For him, Eliot's "socialistic" love has no meaning; he says that Eliot has done for love what the Communists have done for democracy — make it a meaningless word. And there are arguments for Senator Rosewater's position. He is continually being embarrassed and hurt by his son, though Eliot is not really conscious of this. And Eliot's wife, Sylvia, is finally driven insane by Eliot's behavior. Her disease is the textbook case of a new syndrome called "Samaritrophia," and part of a psychological treatise written about her case is quoted in the book. Sylvia is finally unable to care about others. Eliot's fanaticism about universal love drives her to the opposite extreme: she forms a psychological block against love. The doctor who diagnoses her case, however, is unable to describe Eliot's syndrome, except to say that he must stay in Rosewater because "his Destination is there." In other words, Eliot is acting because of inevitability, not of his own free will.

It should be noted that the people whom Eliot is helping are truly in need of some sort of help. Rosewater, Indiana, is a disaster area, primarily because of what the Rosewaters — who have not lived there in years — have done to it. Rosewater County has been wrecked for the benefit of the Rosewater fortune, and the people who live there have been abandoned, left to their own devices. So it is fitting that Eliot's good deeds should be done for their benefit. He believes that these common people are "the salt of the earth" and "the soul of the U.S. infantry." In reality, they are neither. Nor are they, as his father insists, "common criminals." Vonnegut points out that they have neither the motivation nor the cleverness to be successful criminals, though the Moody family, for instance, does have some sort of congenital biological impulse toward committing arson. And it is evident that Eliot is not completely deceived about these people; he predicts that the newborn Moody twins, Foxcroft and Melody, will grow up to be "firebugs." But he still insists on doing what his father cannot: recognizing them as people.

If the inhabitants of Rosewater County are hopeless, so are Norman Mushari's clients, Fred and Caroline Rosewater of Pisquontuit, Rhode Island. Fred is a suicidally-inclined life insurance salesman; his wife Caroline is pretending to social status by having an affair with a rich lesbian, Amanita Buntline. These Rosewaters never suspect their relationship to Senator Rosewater until Norman Mushari tells them about it. And Mushari arrives just in time to prevent Fred from putting an end to his pointless existence by hanging himself in the basement. Fred and Caroline do, in fact, have a legitimate claim to the Rosewater fortune. They are descendants of noble, patriotic George Rosewater, who was duped out of his share of the family's holdings during the Civil War by his unscrupulous older brother Noah, Senator Rosewater's grandfather. The history of the Rosewater family, as narrated in a letter which Eliot leaves to his appointed heir, is a satire on the founding of great American fortunes. The Rosewater millions were not obtained by honest, self-sacrificing hard work; they were amassed by lying, cheating, and self-righteousness. Eliot sarcastically describes the family motto as "Grab much too much, or you'll get nothing at all." This seems to be an apt description of the philosophies of Noah Rosewater, Senator Rosewater, and Norman Mushari. As for Fred and Caroline, the main beneficiaries of Mushari's plot, they are merely pawns in his game; Mushari must make them rich in order to make himself rich. They are, of course, eager to go along with Mushari's scheme, for they subscribe to the American notion that wealth brings happiness and meaning into life. This proposition is discredited in the book by the example of Stewart Buntline, Amanita's husband. Buntline has adapted himself so well to a life of idleness that he has become somewhat of a vegetable. His wife is a domineering lesbian (her name,

Amanita, is the name of a genus of poisonous mushrooms) and his daughter Lila sells pornography to her schoolmates. His life is no more meaningful and rewarding than that of Fred Rosewater or even of Diana Moon Glampers, an illiterate spinster in Rosewater, Indiana, whom Vonnegut describes as being almost "too dumb to live."

Perhaps the only person in the novel who is leading a full, meaningful life is a minor character, Harry Pena. Unlike the other characters, Harry is satisfied with his work (he is a fisherman), has a sense of his own worth as an individual, and is satisfied to be what he is. In short, he is an example of the Protestant work ethic at its best. Vonnegut does seem to believe that purposeful employment gives a man a sense of fulfillment. However, he does not seem to believe that selling insurance (like Fred Rosewater) or being a U.S. Senator (like Lister Ames Rosewater) are meaningful occupations. Harry is a romantic figure: he is strong, self-sufficient, and in constant contact with the forces of nature. He is also doomed by society. His profession, like many others, is being automated out of existence, and once it is gone, we can predict that he will become another meaningless cipher, like the people of Rosewater County. Vonnegut exhibits little faith in the American dream of each individual leading a purposeful, dignified life. In the rare instances when it does work (Harry Pena, for example), it is rapidly coming to an end. America is just another failed Utopia, an attempt at a perfect society which did not work.

In a larger sense, what Eliot Rosewater is trying to do is to restore the Utopian aspects of the American dream by restoring self-respect to as many individuals as possible. He is described by his father's psychiatrist, in a parody of Freudian psychology, as having sexual drives toward Utopia. He fails, of course. The pressure of his own altruism, of his wife's divorce suit against him, and of his father's pleas that he come to his senses finally drive him insane, and he is taken to an asylum in Indianapolis. He does, however, regain his sanity in time to foil Norman Mushari's plans to have the family fortune transferred to his clients. And the way in which this is finally accomplished is a compromise between his own idealism and his father's hard-headed pragmatism. He simply legitimizes all the children in Rosewater County whom Norman Mushari, in an attempt to discredit his "saintliness," has accused him of fathering. In so doing, he acknowledges their rights to trusteeship of the Rosewater Foundation in the event of his being found legally incompetent. He pays Fred and Caroline a token amount and is rid of them.

In devising this simple, direct solution to his dilemma, Eliot rejects the advice of his hero, science fiction writer Kilgore Trout. Trout's argument for Eliot's sanity presents a sort of idealistic, optimistic moral to the book: Eliot's work in Rosewater County was a sociological experiment, proving that people need all the uncritical love they can get. His ability to provide this love, if only on a short-term basis, demonstrates that there is still hope for mankind. The theory is attractive, but to subscribe to it wholeheartedly is to ignore the damage that Eliot has done to Sylvia and his father. In addition, it overlooks the sort of rancor that remains in Rosewater County after he leaves.

Trout, like Eliot, is an idealistic dreamer. His novels had a great influence on Eliot's ideas, yet, like Eliot, he is a failure. He is described as an ironic Christ-figure, and he supports himself by working in a trading-stamp redemption center. Throughout the book, plot summaries of his novels provide a sort of counterpoint to the main action; one of them, *2BR02B*, states the central question with which *God Bless You, Mr. Rosewater* is concerned: "What in hell are people *for*?" The question remains unanswered; each individual must answer it for himself.

In the final analysis, our perception of the novel depends on what we decide about the main character, Mr. Rosewater. Is he a saint or is he a crackpot? Vonnegut seems to be saying that, like all human beings, he is a little of both.

SLAUGHTERHOUSE-FIVE

Slaughterhouse-Five is structurally the most intricate of Vonnegut's writings. It tells, chronologically, the story of Billy

Pilgrim's capture and imprisonment by the Germans during World War II, but interspersed with this chronological story are incidents from Billy's life on Earth before and after the war, and from his fantasy voyage to the planet Tralfamadore, where he is exhibited in an intergalactic zoo. Billy has "come unstuck in time": he has begun to move forward and backward through his life in a random sequence of events. During his lifetime, he simultaneously lives the mundane life of an optometrist in Ilium, New York, and, in a time-warp, is mated to movie star Montana Wildhack on Tralfamadore. So Billy, in his "time-tripping," moves from event to event from his life on Earth and occasionally finds himself on Tralfamadore; he has no control over this time-travel. The only constant point of time-reference in the novel is the chronological sequence of events during World War II, which are the central part of the plot.

Billy's "time-tripping" is, like the visit to Tralfamadore, a science fiction element in the novel, which contrasts with the apparent realism of the scenes from Billy's life. But, more important, it is a structural device which allows Vonnegut to juxtapose scenes from Billy's life for maximum effect. In addition, this elaborate structure is enclosed within a wider framework: in the first and last chapters, the novelist himself appears, telling about the story he is writing and about the events which led to his writing it. Vonnegut himself is also present in some of the prison camp scenes. Thus point-of-view in the novel is complex and somewhat problematical: we have an omniscient narrator who sees and describes not only the characters' actions, but also their thoughts and motives; yet, at the same time, this narrator appears as a minor, and necessarily limited, character in the plot of the novel. Vonnegut seems to be reserving the right to pull the reader out of the context of his story in order to point out to the reader that it is, after all, only fiction and that the author is in control. In effect, Vonnegut is a central character in his own novel, and he assists the reader in the first chapter by giving a biography of himself and explaining how he came to write the novel.

Much of the novel, Vonnegut tells us, is autobiographical. The central plot line — Billy's war experiences — is a fictionalized account of Vonnegut's war experiences. The remaining details of Billy Pilgrim's life are fictional, as, of course, are his time-trips and his visit to Tralfamadore (an experience not directly related to his traveling in time). Apart from his war experiences and his science fiction exploits, Billy's life is really quite conventional and bland. He was "a funny-looking child who became a funny-looking youth"; he went through the war, had a nervous breakdown, married, became an optometrist, had two children, and became moderately rich. Vonnegut summarizes these events in chronological order at the beginning of Billy's story, then returns to them from time to time as Billy travels back and forth through his life.

The first unconventional acts of Billy's otherwise apparently mundane life occur in 1968, when he begins to reveal details of his trip to Tralfamadore and his time travels. (This is shortly before the "fictional present" – if the book can be said to have one – from which Vonnegut narrates the story.) When Billy begins to tell his story, he has just recovered from a near-fatal plane crash and his wife has just died. Thus Billy's story is received as though it were the ramblings of a prematurely senile man. But because of his ability to travel forward as well as backward in time, Billy knows that his story will eventually be accepted. (Despite his ability to see into the future, the only event of Billy's later life that is narrated is his death, by assassination, in 1976.)

Billy's time-tripping began shortly before his capture by the Germans in 1944, but he was not to understand what was happening to him until it was explained by the Tralfamadorians in 1966. Billy's relationship to time is much different from that of the Tralfamadorians. He lives each moment of time separately, like most human beings; it is simply the sequence of events which has become disarranged for him. The Tralfamadorians live all moments simultaneously. For them, time has no movement; there is no past, present, or future – there is only one eternal moment.

The Tralfamadorians' perception of time as a unity gives them a peculiar philosophy, which they gradually teach to Billy.

Everything that happens *must* happen. Nothing can be done to change it because each moment is structured in its own particular way — it always has been and always will be. This ties in with Vonnegut's comment in the first chapter that it is as pointless to write an anti-war novel as it is to write an anti-glacier novel. There is no way to stop the inevitable. The effect of this knowledge on Billy results in a sort of resigned Stoicism: if one cannot change anything, one must learn to accept it. The Tralfamadorians also have some advice for Billy in this regard: humans should learn to concentrate on the good moments and ignore the bad ones. Unfortunately, this advice is futile because the Tralfamadorians cannot understand the human concept of time. A human cannot pick and choose; he must live each moment, pleasant or unpleasant, as it comes along. And this is especially true of Billy; he has no way of predicting his next moment.

The Tralfamadorian outlook on time also supplies Vonnegut with the catch-phrase which he uses as a motif throughout the novel: "So it goes." This, he says, is a Tralfamadorian expression used when looking at a corpse; the Tralfamadorians know that, however wretched a person is at a certain moment, in other moments he is fine. But when used by an Earthling like Vonnegut — and he uses it in the book whenever he refers to someone dying, about one hundred times in all — it is more a matter of there being nothing else more meaningful to say — like the birds saying "*Poo-tee-weet?*" after a massacre. It becomes a mannerism, a gesture, a hopeless shrug in the face of the inevitable.

Vonnegut uses Billy's time-tripping to juxtapose events in three different contexts: the horrors of the war, the bland complacency of Billy's "normal" life after the war, and the idyll with Montana Wildhack on Tralfamadore. Frequently, the juxtapositions are used for comic effect. In one sequence, Billy moves from the Tralfamadorian zoo to his wedding night with Valencia. When he gets up to go to the bathroom, he finds himself in a German prison camp, looking for the latrine. When he leaves the latrine, he finds himself back with Valencia, having just returned from the bathroom. He goes to bed, falls asleep, and awakens on a train on the way to his father's funeral — with an erection. Here, not only time has become jumbled, but so have cause and effect. Billy's erection in 1944 is caused by his wedding night in 1948. A few years later, a similar thing happens: he travels from his first night with Montana Wildhack in 1967 to a night in 1968 when he had a wet dream.

Sometimes the events in a sequence are thematically ordered. Billy goes from a discussion of literature with the Tralfamadorians, through two brief scenes from his twelfth year, to the German prison camp, where the Englishmen put on a satire of *Cinderella*. During the play, he becomes violently ill and is taken to the hospital, where he is watched over by Edgar Derby. Derby is reading *The Red Badge of Courage*. Then Billy travels to a psychiatric ward in 1948, where he discusses *The Brothers Karamazov* and the writings of Kilgore Trout (a minor character in this novel and a favorite Vonnegut stock character) with Eliot Rosewater. The literary references throughout this sequence serve to unify it and to emphasize the connection between the literary conversations with which it begins and ends.

But Vonnegut's main purpose in juxtaposing events out of context is to transpose the war with the course of peacetime life and with the fantasies of science fiction. The war, especially the catastrophic bombing of Dresden, is the key to this book. And the war is a nightmare for Billy. From the very first, he is out of place in the war. He is not a soldier, but a victim. He has not been issued any equipment when he gets lost behind German lines; and when he loses a heel from his civilian shoes, he bobs up and down when he walks, like a puppet. In effect, he is a puppet, for he has lost all control of himself, even his will to stay alive.

Billy's appearance is so ludicrous that after his capture the Germans use him in propaganda films showing how ill-equipped and pathetic the American army is. But things get worse for him: when he arrives at the prison camp, he is given a fur-collared civilian's coat, several sizes too small. And he soon acquires, out of necessity, a pair of silver boots, a muff, and an azure blue toga, made out of a curtain. He is not trying to look funny; he is trying to survive, but when he finally arrives in Dresden, he is berated by an English-speaking surgeon for the costume which fate has given him. Billy has become a sort of ironic clown, who finds himself playing a role in a tragedy.

Nothing about the war seems to function as it should. When Billy is first cast adrift behind German lines, he is picked up by two scouts and an antitank gunner named Roland Weary. Weary, who claims to be saving Billy's life, actually delights in torturing him, and Billy is only saved from Weary by being captured by the Germans. The two scouts, who are good soldiers, are killed; Billy and Weary, two misfits, survive. Later, in Dresden after the bombing, Edgar Derby is shot for stealing a teapot, yet Billy manages to keep a two-carat diamond which he found in the lining of his coat. There is no sense to the system of rewards and punishment, nor is there any justice. And, to Vonnegut, the greatest injustice of all is the bombing of Dresden. Dresden was considered an "open" city; it had no direct connection with the German war effort. It was bombed as an ultimatum to the Germans to surrender, much as the Japanese cities of Hiroshima and Nagasaki were destroyed by the atomic bomb — as a warning to Japan.

In a sense, *Slaughterhouse-Five* is an apocalyptic novel — that is, it ends with the bombing of Dresden. Many of the events of the novel occur later, chronologically speaking. But the bombing is the climax of the novel, the event toward which all the other events in the novel have been working. It is the final mark of man's inhumanity. Yet this event is juxtaposed with another, much more tender scene: on Tralfamadore, Montana Wildhack is nursing the baby she has had by Billy. And this scene is preceded by one in which Billy begins to announce his discoveries about the nature of time in an attempt to alleviate the suffering of mankind. So even amid the destruction, life goes on — perhaps everything balances out in the end.

The two slogans which Vonnegut uses as illustrations in the book are of some thematic importance. The first is engraved on a locket hanging between Montana Wildhack's breasts and is also enscribed on a plaque hanging in Billy's office: "God grant me the serenity to accept the things I cannot change, courage to change the things I can, and wisdom always to tell the difference." In the context of the book, this slogan is ironic, for, as Vonnegut observes, "Among the things Billy Pilgrim could not change were the past, the present, and the future." In the Tralfamadorian time-scheme, nothing can be changed because every moment is always structured in its own particular way. What the slogan actually means is: accept everything, for you can change nothing. And it is in the serenity that leads to this acceptance, his gift from the Tralfamadorians, that Billy thinks of the other slogan, which is to be his epitaph (and Vonnegut's): "Everything was beautiful, and nothing hurt."

HAPPY BIRTHDAY, WANDA JUNE

Vonnegut's play *Happy Birthday, Wanda June* is loosely based on the last book of Homer's *Odyssey*. In this poem, Odysseus returns home from the Trojan War to find his wife, Penelope, besieged by suitors. With the help of his son, Telemachus, he slaughters the suitors, reclaims his wife, and restores peace and order to the kingdom. Vonnegut says that he found Odysseus' behavior "cruelly preposterous" and wrote a play about it, which he titled *Penelope. Happy Birthday, Wanda June* is an outgrowth of that play.

The "Odysseus" of this play is Harold Ryan, whom Vonnegut admits is modeled on the worst aspects of the novelist Ernest Hemingway. Ryan is a professional soldier and big game hunter —a braggart, a male chauvinist, and a general all-around bully. He has been missing and presumed dead for eight years, along with his partner, Colonel Looseleaf Harper, who dropped the atomic bomb on Nagasaki. Ryan's wife is appropriately named Penelope and she has two suitors: Doctor Norbert Woodly and a vacuum cleaner salesman named Herb Shuttle. Harold's son, Paul, despises both of these men and keeps warning them that his father is going to return. Paul, who is too young to remember Harold, worships his father, but this situation changes as the play progresses, after Harold and Looseleaf Harper return home on Harold's birthday.

The play revolves around Harold's conflicts, past and present, with the other characters. During the course of the action, he manages to alienate everyone. The present action, it should be noted, is observed by a chorus of three "ghosts," who have formed a Harold Ryan Fan Club in Heaven. The Fan Club is ironic; their official jacket is pink, with a yellow stripe down the back. It is composed of two people: Major Siegfried von Konigswald, "The Beast of Yugoslavia," whom Harold killed during World War II, and Wanda June, whose birthday cake was bought for Harold after she was killed by an ice cream truck. Harold's third wife, Mildred, whom Harold's premature ejaculation drove to alcoholism, refuses to join the club.

The major opposition in the play is between Harold and Doctor Woodly, who is a pacifist. Woodly and Penelope have become secretly engaged, much to the disgust of Harold, Paul, and Herb Shuttle, all of whom consider him a coward. Thus Woodly and Harold are opposed—in dramatic terms, as rivals for Penelope's love, and in thematic terms, as representatives of conflicting ideologies. Yet neither side can really be said to win; neither Harold nor Woodly emerges as the hero of the play. In their final confrontation, Harold is "destroyed" by Woodly's charge that he is no better than a clown. His self-respect and honor have been taken from him and, with them, goes his killer instinct: he is incapable of killing Woodly—or even himself. But Harold does manage to destroy Woodly's self-righteous idealism when he forces him to plead for his life. Woodly has to admit to himself what he had denied all along: he is a coward. (Ironically, however, Penelope found this attractive in him, compared to Harold's bravura. It is because Woodly insists on facing Harold on his own terms that she turns against him.) At the end of the play, both Harold and Woodly have left behind their old lives and must search for new beginnings.

Penelope's other suitor, Herb Shuttle, is a weight lifter and a sports fan and fancies himself a he-man. His main attraction to

Penelope seems to be that she is Harold Ryan's wife: when Harold returns, Shuttle's affection for Penelope is quickly transferred to Harold. And after Penelope leaves Harold, Shuttle becomes a sort of housewife to Harold, Looseleaf, and Paul. His comments at this point betray the latent sexual nature of his attraction to Harold: "If *I* were married to him, *I* sure wouldn't walk out." Harold tolerates Shuttle only because he can make fun of him. When he is through with him, he publicly humiliates him and throws him out. Shuttle's reaction to this is characteristically weak: he tells Harold, "You—you aren't going to have any *friends* left, if you don't watch out." Shuttle is really a weakling, basking in the reflected glory of his heroes, and Harold, recognizing this, has deep contempt for him.

Colonel Looseleaf Harper is a more attractive figure than Harold, Woodly, or Shuttle, despite the fact that he is somewhat scatterbrained and inarticulate. Like Harold, he is recognized as a hero. But, unlike Harold, he does not understand why this is so; he takes no particular pride in his accomplishments. He is honestly confused about his situation; like many of Vonnegut's protagonists, he is a powerless man who has simply reacted to forces beyond his control. In the opening scene, when asked to say something about killing, he responds: "Jesus—I dunno. You know. What the heck. Who knows?" And his only response to Penelope's mention of his having killed 74,000 people by dropping the atomic bomb on Nagasaki is: "I dunno, boy. . . . It was a bitch." But toward the end of the play, he finally—fifteen years too late—makes a judgment about his action. Harold tells him that dropping the bomb was "the one direct, decisive, intelligent act of your life!" Harper, after some consideration, observes that it might have been—if he had chosen *not* to drop the bomb. He might have chosen life over death, but he did not. "I sent 'em to Heaven instead," he observes," —and I don't think there *is* one." He did not make a choice at the time; he merely carried out orders. His choice comes too late to save the citizens of Nagasaki, but, for Harper, it comes as a moment of self-realization: "Anybody who'd drop an atom bomb on a city has to be pretty dumb." He has finally spoken for himself, made his own choice, and in the process he has rejected Harold and Harold's values.

The real protagonist of the play is, as the original title implied, Penelope. Like Looseleaf, she has spent her life dominated by others; in the end, she breaks free. When she met Harold, she was an ignorant carhop; he quickly molded her into the sort of woman he wanted her to be. During his absence, she has become educated and independent of him. She falls under the influence of Woodly's pacificistic ideas, but, ironically, she understands them better than he does himself. She realizes that in risking his life by confronting Harold, Woodly is actually compromising his principles and reacting on Harold's terms. In insisting on defending his honor, he becomes no better than Harold, "no better than the dumbest general in the Pentagon." Now she understands that his principles, like Harold's heroism, were merely a false front. She is the real hero of the confrontation between Harold and Woodly because she realizes what it means and has the good sense to be terrified.

Vonnegut uses the scenes with the "ghosts" in "Heaven" as an ironic commentary on the main action of the play. The Heaven described by Wanda June is patently absurd: it is simply a carnival, a never-never land where all desires are fulfilled immediately. Everyone is thankful to whoever sent them there: the "Harold Ryan Fan Club" is to consist of those whose death Harold was involved with. And everyone is welcome: even Major von Konigswald is there, matter-of-factly commenting upon the various tortures, executions, and murders he assisted with. This sort of Heaven would justify killing, but its absurdity serves to underscore Looseleaf Harper's comment, "I sent 'em to Heaven instead—and I don't think there *is* one."

The abrupt juxtaposition of realism in the main plot of the play with the fantasy of the scenes in Heaven is a distancing technique, removing the audience from any direct identification with the characters in the play. The play is concerned primarily with ideas, not emotions, and the audience must periodically be forced to sit back and think about what is happening. The only intrusion of the "ghosts" into the "real" world of the play is when they appear onstage at the climax to witness Harold's suicide attempt; their presence undercuts the reality of the scene.

Another example of Vonnegut's use of "alienation effects" in the play is having the actors step momentarily out of role, to address the audience directly. This happens when Harold asks, "Who the hell is Wanda June?" just before the first scene in Heaven, and, most notably, at the beginning of the play, when the four main characters appear onstage and discuss their roles. In effect, the audience is being told at the very beginning that they are not to consider this play as a serious representation of real life.

What, then, is the play? It is, above all, a reassessment of the role of the "hero," pointing out that killing is not something that one should admire a man for. By making fun of death and Heaven, it points out that death is a serious matter, indeed. And it emphasizes that those who are willing to die for their principles are as foolish as those who are willing to kill for theirs. As Vonnegut points out in the introduction to *Mother Night,* "When you're dead, you're dead." Life itself is the final value; nothing else really matters.

BREAKFAST OF CHAMPIONS

Breakfast of Champions is, beyond a doubt, the most outrageous and absurd of all Vonnegut's writings. He also claims that it is the last. Referring to his books as "puppet shows," he renounces them and uses this, his final book, as an occasion to clear his mind of them and to set his characters free.

The book is a collection of graffiti, statistics, facts, opinions, advertising slogans, and plot summaries of some of Kilgore Trout's novels, loosely strung together by two intersecting stories. One of the two stories concerns Kilgore Trout, Vonnegut's alter ego from *God Bless You, Mr. Rosewater* and *Slaughterhouse-Five;* the other story concerns Dwayne Hoover, a Pontiac dealer from Midland City who is slowly going insane. Vonnegut describes them as "two lonesome, skinny, fairly old white men on a planet which was dying fast."

Trout's story begins with an invitation to an arts festival in Midland City in 1972, his encounter with Dwayne Hoover, and his meeting with his creator, Kurt Vonnegut, Jr. Trout is a prolific but unknown writer; at the time of his invitation, he has written 117 novels and 2,000 short stories, but has received nothing for them. Most of them have been published by pornography publishers, with obscene illustrations which have nothing to do with the text. Trout's works are cynical observations about humanity, disguised as science fiction. Trout's invitation to the arts festival is the work of the eccentric millionaire, Eliot Rosewater. Rosewater has bribed the chairman of the festival to invite Trout by offering, in exchange, the loan of an El Greco painting.

Most of this plot concerns Trout's preparations for the arts festival and his cross-country odyssey to Midland City. We follow him across the country from New York City — where he is mugged after leaving a pornographic movie (the money he has been given by the festival committee is stolen) — to his eventual arrival in Midland City. Apart from the mugging, there are no events of any real consequence on this trip; what is important takes place in Trout's mind and in the narrator's descriptions of what he is thinking. Much of this story consists of plot summaries of Trout's novels. These are either remembered by Trout or recounted by Vonnegut in describing Trout's reactions to what he sees. One plot summary, however, is narrated to Trout by a truck driver who picks him up; the driver read the story years before, in a jail in Georgia, where he found it in a magazine that was to be used as toilet paper. He does not know that Trout wrote the story and Trout does not claim it as his own.

Trout's stories form an integral part of the book and add greatly to its complexity, for each of the stories is somehow related to themes which Vonnegut explores in the larger context of the novel. One of the stories, particularly, is of crucial importance to the plot of *Breakfast of Champions*: it provides the final impetus which drives Dwayne Hoover insane.

Dwayne Hoover is a successful businessman, who has made himself a success by hard work and cleverness. His life has been comfortable, but not particularly happy. His son is a homosexual, who plays piano at the Holiday Inn; his wife, years before, committed suicide by eating Drāno. He is having a continuing affair with his secretary, Francine Pefko, whose husband was killed in Vietnam. Dwayne's insanity is unmotivated; Vonnegut attributes it to "bad chemicals" in his body, over which he has no control. If Trout's story is an outward journey across the country, Dwayne's is an inward journey from semi-sanity to madness. As the book progresses, he comes gradually closer to a breakdown, until he is finally pushed over the brink by reading Kilgore Trout's novel, *Now It Can Be Told.*

These two stories are told chronologically, in alternating segments. The main purpose of the alternation seems to be to contrast the two lives, which seem to have absolutely nothing in common. Yet throughout the novel, Vonnegut foreshadows the encounter which will take place between the two men. The reader knows what will occur; the only question is *why?*

The book which Kilgore Trout gives Dwayne to read, in the lounge at the Holiday Inn, is written as though it were a message from the Creator of the Universe to an experimental being. This being is the only one in the universe to have free will. Everyone else, including the Creator himself, is a machine. This is just the "message" that Dwayne has been looking for. Earlier in the day, in a motel in neighboring Shepherdstown, he asked Francine to tell him "what life is all about." She suggested that he talk to the artists in town for the festival. So, in his unbalanced state of mind, he takes Trout's book literally: he has free will, everyone else is a machine. And he goes berserk, injuring eleven people. Among these, Kilgore Trout has his ring finger bitten off; Bunny Hoover, Dwayne's son, has his face pushed into the keyboard of his piano and severely cut; and Francine Pefko is badly beaten. It is this incident, Vonnegut tells us, that will lead Kilgore Trout to become recognized as a pioneer in the field of mental health — because of his formulation of the proposition stated on his tombstone: "We are healthy only to the extent that our ideas are humane."

The real protagonist of the novel, however, is neither Kilgore Trout nor Dwayne Hoover: it is Vonnegut himself. He appears as a character toward the end of the novel and observes the confrontation between Trout and Hoover. In addition, he is present throughout the novel, intruding into the action, explaining details, and constantly reminding us that he is writing the novel. In the Preface, Vonnegut describes his novel as "a sidewalk strewn with junk"; it is strewn with the "trash" in his mind in an attempt to purge himself of it. He feels that he has no culture and, in honor of his fiftieth birthday, he wants to start over. Hence, both the title and subtitle of the book are examples of the "trash" he is getting rid of; they are advertising slogans, "Breakfast of Champions" and "Goodbye Blue Monday." Much of the book is a satirical description of American history and culture, written as if it were a child's primer from sometime after the fall of America. Vonnegut explains, in simple and direct terms, the various symbols and obsessions of America to someone from a society which does not share them — someone from an indefinite, future Utopia founded on the principles of Kilgore Trout.

In the Epilogue to the book, Vonnegut confronts Trout directly, as his creator, and tells him what is in store for him. He tells Trout that he is only a character in a novel, then frees him from control. And Trout, having found his creator, reacts pathetically; he calls after the departing Vonnegut, *"Make me young, make me young, make me young!"* But the plea, apparently, goes unheeded.

Ironically, Vonnegut stands in the same relationship to Trout as Trout did to Dwayne Hoover. Hoover saw Trout as his creator, a man who had given to him alone the gift of free will. Vonnegut *is* Trout's creator and gives him — along with all his other characters, who are not told of the gift — free will. Yet Hoover's illusion of free will drives him mad; and it is not free will that Trout wants — but youth.

If we see Vonnegut as the real protagonist of the novel, then the climax of the book is not the encounter between Kilgore Trout and Dwayne Hoover, but an incident just before it. It is an impromptu speech given by the minimal painter Rabo Karabekian (whom Vonnegut had intended to be a negative character).

Vonnegut mentions in the Preface that he has a tendency to see people either as machines (as in *Now It Can Be Told)* or as test tubes full of chemicals (as in his descriptions of Dwayne Hoover's disease). Karabekian's speech offers an alternative vision of humanity which, he says, amounts to a rebirth. Karabekian begins by asking a question about a local celebrity, who is a swimming champion: "What kind of a man would turn his daughter into an outboard motor?" This question implies a denial of man's mechanistic nature; it implies an alternative. Karabekian states the alternative, describing St. Anthony in his painting: each individual is an "unwavering band of light." This revelation impresses the author; it is the answer he has been looking for, the key to a culture which will replace the one he is discarding. Through the unlikely character of Karabekian, he has found an alternative to his own pessimism and cynicism: what is sacred is life itself.

Perhaps the book may best be seen as the author's grappling with cynicism and despair and — finally — arriving at a solution. On the way to the solution, however, a good deal of dark humor rises from the cynicism which Vonnegut is casting off. Vonnegut uses the "trash" of American society, in words and crude drawings, to make the point that society is sick and needs a new vision. His ability to find this vision is a sign that there may still be some hope for society.

SPECIAL TOPICS

There are a number of key themes which run throughout Vonnegut's works. A few of these, because of their importance, deserve special consideration, for they are best understood as they occur in the varying contexts of the different books.

FREE WILL, PREDESTINATION, AND THE ABSURD

In Vonnegut's universe, man is typically the victim of forces beyond his control and understanding. The *karass* in *Cat's Cradle* "does God's will" without ever knowing what it is; Howard W. Campbell, Jr. spews propaganda he doesn't believe in order to convey messages he doesn't understand in *Mother Night;* Paul Proteus in *Player Piano* is a puppet, manipulated by two opposing political factions. Even if a character knows what the future holds for him, as do Winston Niles Rumfoord in *The Sirens of Titan* and Billy Pilgrim in *Slaughterhouse-Five,* he is powerless to alter his destiny in any way. Because of man's powerlessness, the question of free will is irrelevant. Man cannot alter his destiny of his own volition; everything that happens must happen, and man is powerless to change it. Yet there is no concept of events being predestined: predestination implies an order and pattern to events. And there is no particular order in the universe. All is chaos; what happens, happens at random. There is no informing wisdom, no God; there is only "accident," "chance," or "Fate."

The human predicament is that man attempts to make order out of chaos. The universe is absurd, unintelligible, but man must pretend that he understands it and must try to exert some control over it. He has two options. He may try to alter the course of events through the force of his will, by using science or magic; or he may attempt to understand the future through understanding the will of God, through religion. These constructs are absurd because they rely upon free will and predestination, neither of which really is applicable to the situation. But man must try, even though he is doomed to failure.

WHAT ARE PEOPLE FOR?

In one of Kilgore Trout's novels, an old man who is about to die hopes that he will go to Heaven so that he can find an answer to the question "What the hell are people *for?*" Man must feel that he is serving some purpose. In *Player Piano,* the revolt occurs because the common people feel useless; they have lost their dignity and their feeling of usefulness. In all of Vonnegut's novels, characters are "used" by other characters, by Fate, or—in *Breakfast of Champions*—by the author of the novel. Vonnegut even supplies a couple of facetious answers to this matter. In *The Sirens of Titan*, the purpose of thousands of years of human history is revealed to be the delivery of a spare part for Salo's spaceship. In *Breakfast of Champions*, Kilgore Trout answers the graffiti "What is the purpose of life?" with "To be the eyes and ears and conscience of the Creator of the Universe, you fool!" But neither of these answers is really satisfactory. Clearly, the only purpose of life *is* life. What people are for is to be the best human beings they possibly can. There is no need to look for meaning or purpose beyond that; existence is enough in itself.

LOVE

For Vonnegut, love seems to be a force of good that can sometimes be the cause of evil. Campbell's love for Helga in *Mother Night* is good, in itself, yet it insulates him from the world to the extent that he becomes a contributing factor in the slaughter of millions of Jews by the Nazis. In *God Bless You, Mr. Rosewater*, the situation is reversed: Eliot Rosewater's "selfless" love for the world at large causes his wife's insanity and is a source of deep anguish to his father. Love has two aspects, the selfish and the unselfish, and it is never clear just which Rosewater's is. In *The Sirens of Titan*, Rumfoord's love for the world causes him to invent a new religion, based on peace and equality. Yet his means of bringing this religion about involves the slaughter of thousands of innocents. Vonnegut seems to be sentimental about the possibilities of love, but cynical about its actual practice.

BEING AND BECOMING

According to Vonnegut, a man usually has no choice but to be what he is; he is not given the will to change himself. There are, however, notable examples of exceptions to this rule in Vonnegut's works: Luke Lubbock of *Player Piano* is able to be what he dresses as. But most men do not adapt so easily. Vonnegut warns in the introduction to *Mother Night* that "we are what we pretend to be, so we must be careful what we pretend to be." Campbell, in that novel, becomes a war criminal by pretending to be a Nazi; in *Cat's Cradle*, McCabe and Bokonon find themselves becoming the roles they have assumed. Each role requires something of the player; and, eventually, the player becomes the role. There is also a positive side to the process: man must adapt to his circumstances if he is to survive. Penelope, in *Happy Birthday, Wanda June*, says, "We adapt to what there is to adapt to." In *Breakfast of Champions*, Vonnegut suggests as an epitaph for Wayne Hoobler, the black jailbird, what seems to be the highest compliment he can pay: "He adapted to what there was to adapt to."

NATURAL DEPRAVITY VS. NATURAL GOODNESS

Vonnegut is proud of the fact that none of his books have villains, but it should be noted that none of them really have heroes. Even the Nazis in *Mother Night* are not purely evil, and even Mr. Rosewater, who loves all mankind, is not purely good. Man is neither good, nor evil: he is a mixture of the two. The situation is best summarized by Eliot Rosewater: "I love you sons of bitches. . . ."

QUESTIONS FOR REVIEW

1. Discuss the theme of free will in *The Sirens of Titan* or *Cat's Cradle*.

2. Compare Eliot Rosewater's concept of love with that of his father.

3. What is the significance of Billy's time-travel in *Slaughterhouse-Five*, in terms of theme or structure?

4. What is the significance of the title *Player Piano*?

5. Discuss the relationship of Vonnegut to Kilgore Trout and Dwayne Hoover in *Breakfast of Champions*.

6. What is the role of God in Bokononism?

7. How genuine is Dr. Woodly's pacifism in *Happy Birthday, Wanda June*?

8. Discuss role-playing and reality in *Mother Night* or *Cat's Cradle*.

9. What is a chrono-synclastic infundibulum?

10. Explain the statement "We adapt to what there is to adapt to."

11. Compare the Tralfamadorians in *The Sirens of Titan* with those in *Slaughterhouse-Five*.

12. Compare the Church of God the Utterly Indifferent with Bokononism, as Utopian religions.

13. Compare and contrast science and religion in *Cat's Cradle*.

14. Discuss the meaning of the phrase "So it goes."

15. What the hell are people for?

SELECTED BIBLIOGRAPHY

WORKS BY VONNEGUT

Novels

Player Piano. New York: Delacorte, 1952.

The Sirens of Titan. New York: Delacorte, 1959.

Mother Night. New York: Delacorte, 1961.

Cat's Cradle. New York: Delacorte, 1963.

God Bless You, Mr. Rosewater, or Pearls Before Wine. New York: Delacorte, 1965.

Slaughterhouse-Five, or the Children's Crusade. New York: Delacorte, 1969.

Breakfast of Champions, or Goodbye, Blue Monday. New York: Delacorte, 1973.

Plays

Happy Birthday, Wanda June. New York: Delacorte, 1970.

Between Time and Timbuktu, or Prometheus-5. New York: Dell, 1972.

Collections of Short Stories

Canary in a Cathouse. New York: Delacorte, 1961.

Welcome to the Monkey House. New York: Delacorte, 1970.

WORKS ABOUT VONNEGUT

Benjamin DeMott. "Vonegut's Otherworldly Laughter." *Saturday Review*, 54 (May 1, 1971).

Leslie Fiedler. "The Divine Stupidity of Kurt Vonnegut." *Esquire* (September, 1970).

Jerome Klinkowitz and John Somer. *The Vonnegut Statement.* New York: Delacorte, 1973.

"Kurt Vonnegut, Jr.: A Symposium." *Summary*, 1 (2, 1971).

Peter J. Reed. *Kurt Vonnegut, Jr.* New York: Paperback Library, 1972.

"Vonnegut." *Critique*, 12 (3, 1971).

NOTES

NOTES

NOTES

NOTES

NOTES

NOTES